T0114621

Books by Connie Bertelsen Young

*Signs of The Time*
*Esprit De Corps*
*You're Only Old Once*
*Heart Words*
*The House of You*
*Imperceptible Reality*

# *We Are The* BRANCHES

### and we function better in our churches

## CONNIE BERTELSEN YOUNG

WESTBOW
PRESS®
A DIVISION OF THOMAS NELSON
& ZONDERVAN

WestBow Press books may be ordered through booksellers or by contacting:

WestBow Press
A Division of Thomas Nelson & Zondervan
1663 Liberty Drive
Bloomington, IN 47403
www.westbowpress.com
844-714-3454

ISBN: 979-8-3850-0369-3 (sc)
ISBN: 979-8-3850-0368-6 (e)

Library of Congress Control Number: 2023913721

Print information available on the last page.

WestBow Press rev. date: 08/25/2023

# Contents

*I am the vine;*
*you are the branches.*
*If you remain in me and I in you,*
*you will bear much fruit;*
*apart from me you can do nothing.*
*(John 15:5 NIV)*

## *Dedication*

Dedicated with appreciation to all who faithfully help to keep the Church running smoothly, especially those who continually labored despite the risks involved with public ministry during the scourge of the Corona Virus Pandemic. Thank you!

# Introduction

Along with many other institutions, the Church took a devastating hit from the Covid Virus pandemic. As fear escalated, amplified by frightening media and medical reports, millions of people on earth were inhibited from living freely in close connection with their fellow man. At this writing, statistics indicate that over 676,108,561 people have tested positive and have experienced the symptoms of the Corona Virus, while approximately 6,770,509 people have died from its ramifications.[1]

There has been much speculation by the Christian community about why the whole earth experienced this plague. Some believe it was a result of ignoring God, showing similarity to the plagues that the nation of Israel suffered due to sin, which we read about in the Old Testament. Others surmise that, because technology allows better reporting of diseases and disasters than records offered from previous centuries, there may have been unjustified panic about that which has always been happening when documentation and warnings were not as available. They have quoted the following verse.

*That which has been is what will be, That which is done*

*is what will be done, And there is nothing new under the sun (Ecclesiastes 1:9 NKJV).*

Others remind us that plagues, along with other worldwide problems, are indicative of the end times. Certainly, all the prophetic indications seen in 2 Timothy 3:1-5 are happening. Notwithstanding, in attempting to determine whether the pandemic experience was due to this or that, Christians may have slid from believing Romans 8:28 and recognizing the perfect judgment of God who can—and does—use every circumstance, problem or obstacle for our good.

We have all seen the repercussions of the Corona Virus, with much of it yet remaining throughout the world. Numerous individuals continue to hide behind their masks or closed doors, hesitating to venture out because of their dread of contamination through association with other people. Sadly, this is affecting the body, soul and spiritual health of us all, and it is especially detrimental to our children.

Before I proceed, I certainly don't attribute *all* the blame for the disturbing decline in worship attendance within our churches to the Corona Virus Pandemic, although it has been used as an excuse. There are other things to consider. The emphasis of this book is not so much the cause for the drop in numbers. Rather, I'm concentrating more on the necessity of remaining within Church life and worship attendance, despite whatever rationalization is used for avoidance.

Statistics show that a lot of people are tired and exhausted,[2] and reports indicate that fatigue is common.[3] Many of us want something to energize ourselves. I suppose it's ironic to mention that assembling ourselves together with other Christians can do a lot more for us than those popular energy drinks or other over-the-counter pick-me-ups we've tried. For instance, various reports estimate that more than 150 million Americans drink about 400 million cups of coffee per day, the equivalent of more than 140 billion cups per year.[4] Still, it's obvious that people remain unsatisfied.

We are made up of body, soul and spirit, and each of these parts is closely related and influenced by the other parts. If we only give care to our bodily needs and desires, the other parts will weaken from lack of attention. This fact is significant to the functioning of our body, but it is also significant to the functioning of the Church, the Body of Christ, because the Church is made up of more than one part, too.

*But in fact God has placed the parts in the body, every one of them, just as he wanted them to be (1 Corinthians 12:18 NIV).*

If some of those parts are neglected or inoperative in the Church, the Church will suffer. A truly committed Christian will determine to obey the call of God and connect with other believers.

Of course, it isn't merely being in the church building that provides all the soul and spirit health for us or for the Body of Christ. Church attendance isn't a magical mixture that tastes sweet, pumps us up and temporarily gratifies. In fact, it should make us uncomfortable on occasion. If we're too comfortable, we probably aren't growing. Nevertheless, being physically together with other believers has great value and brings divine blessing that doesn't come other ways, as I will try to explain in the following chapters.

I should mention that the virtual church is a blessed alternative for those who are not physically able to attend church for various reasons, and it is a valuable tool for appealing to the lost who might happen to tune in, but there is something that is accomplished in the physical connection that doesn't happen virtually. In Hebrews 10:25, Paul emphasized the importance of "*not giving up meeting together, as some are in the habit of doing. . . .*" Also, several times in 1 Corinthians, he used the phrase "*when you come together,*"[5] and he repeatedly explained that God's children need a physical gathering.

Catherine Marshall wrote, "No branch can live unless attached to the Vine, and the Vine has not a single branch, but many branches."[6] As branches, we help to bring each other strength and vibrancy.

My friends, Rev. and Mrs. Tim Curtis, love visiting America's national parks. Tim and Diana have shared some fascinating stories about what they've seen and learned from this pastime. One day, Tim elaborated on the interesting root system of California's magnificent Sequoia trees, and he compared it to how Christians are dependent on each other. He explained that we see the mighty Giant Sequoia standing straight and tall, appearing to be self-sustaining, but if we could see beneath the ground, we'd discover these giants of the forest rely on an interesting support system. They have long roots which are intertwined and tightly tangled with other trees for strength, in order to survive.

Like the Giant Sequoia, a Christian was never meant

to go it alone but rather to be firmly intertwined, rooted and grounded in the Foundation of the Family of God.[7] The community of believers is the Christian's support system, and that support system is available to us through regular attendance and fellowship in a local church. Without that support, we become weak and vulnerable. My hope is that, through the following pages, readers will be inspired to see the absolute need for secure placement in a Bible-believing church where you will experience the strength and encouragement that is available as you become well-established in obedience to God's plan.

**Connie Bertelsen Young**

## Note to Readers

Although there are many aspects of the Church that I'm not able to cover in one book, it's important for readers to understand the difference in what I'm writing about when I spell "Church" (with an upper-case "C") and "church" (with a lower-case "c").

When I mention the "Church," I'm referring to the universal Body of Christ. This includes everyone who has received Jesus Christ as their Savior. When I write "church," however, I simply mean the building which is specifically used for the necessary gathering of Christians for worship and fellowship. Although Bible translations may not always distinguish the differences by using upper-case and lower-case letters, I'm using this practice for the sake of the message in this book.

✝

# Chapter 1

# ROOTS

*There shall come forth a Rod from the stem of Jesse, And a Branch shall grow out of his roots (Isaiah 11:1 NKJV).*

The life of the Church began on the day of Pentecost, and the Church was rooted and planted by the Holy Spirit on that meaningful day. This was the very glorious beginning when our branches began to miraculously grow from the Vine, Jesus Christ.

I can see a picture in my mind's eye—like time-lapse photography—of those original life-filled shoots forming, first with those early Christians, and then strong, healthy branches stretching across the earth through the centuries. Quite amazingly, every Christian is joined with those believers. Countless numbers are part of this tremendous growth, since it includes all those who have accepted Jesus Christ as their Savior over the centuries.

Although you may have heard about Pentecost many times, look again at this special event that birthed Christianity, described in the second chapter of the book of Acts, and try to imagine its reverberating impact. If you belong to Jesus Christ, this beginning is where you can trace your roots!

First, there was the sound like the blowing of a violent wind which filled the whole house. You've probably listened to the sound of wind whistling through the trees or puffing against your windows on a wintery day. Depending upon where you live in the world, you know the noise of wind can be astounding. For instance, it can moan, or seem to cry like a baby, and the roar of a hurricane or the racket of a tornado is eardrum-piercingly loud. However, nothing was written about stormy weather, only that there was a *sound* like a violent wind—inside the house!

*The wind blows where it wishes, and you hear the sound of it, but cannot tell where it comes from and where it goes. So is everyone who is born of the Spirit." (John 3:8 NKJV).*

Try to imagine those mysterious tongues of fire, appearing out of nowhere, separating, and then resting on each believer. Were the participants stunned and shaking in their sandals? Do you think it took their breath away, or were they full of peace and weeping with joy?

I don't believe there was the smell of burnt hair or clothing from the tongues of fire, but I believe onlookers saw their faces glowing—like Moses' face shone after being in the presence of God.[8] Meanwhile, even though they probably didn't smell smoke, maybe the lovely scent of the Lord, described in Hosea 14:6, was noticeable.

These were ordinary people who loved and worshiped God. They didn't have a degree in linguistics. They were not polyglots (people fluent in other languages). Yet, as the Holy Spirit fell upon them, they had the extraordinary ability to speak perfectly in other tongues, and they clearly communicated to those in attendance, though they hadn't learned to speak their native languages.

*All of them were filled with the Holy Spirit and began to speak in other tongues as the Spirit enabled them (Acts 2:4 NIV).*

All these things that happened at Pentecost must have amazed and blessed those who participated, but I don't believe this astonishing move of the Spirit would have happened like that if the believers hadn't been together in one place.

One of my primary goals for this book is to show the importance of Christians gathering with other believers in churches. The location, the size, or the type of building may vary, but we need a physical place where we can be together regularly so that the power of God will be magnified and manifested through us. As we worship God and connect with each other in fellowship at our church "house," as they did at that house on that day when the Church was launched, we will also have glorious experiences together as branches, that are uniquely different from when we are alone.

Of course, it's possible for one to experience the Glory of God at any time and at any place. There are arguments from people who think that going to church is unnecessary because of that fact. Nevertheless, I believe that because of the culture in which we live, regular church attendance is the most efficient way in which we can grow, function effectively, and obey the following verse.

*Not forsaking the assembling of ourselves together, as is the manner of some, but exhorting one another, and so much the more as you see the Day approaching (Hebrews 10:25 NKJV).*

Jonathan Leeman wrote, "Sometimes people like to say that a church is a people, not a place. It's slightly more accurate to say that a church is a people assembled in a place."[9]

Admittedly, the Church that we read about in the New Testament is not alluding to a physical structure. However, the buildings which we now distinguish as churches, have a very prominent part in Christian life today, even though the true Church is not defined by a physical place. Still, we find the word "churches" used in the Bible when various groups or gatherings are mentioned. For instance, we read that Paul addressed specific letters to individual churches, yet, legitimately, there is only one Church, and he was careful to teach that fact.

*But now indeed there are many members, yet one body (1 Corinthians 12:20 NKJV).*

One day when Jesus was conversing with the disciples, he asked them an important question. Peter's answer to that question was, and is, requisite in becoming a member of the Scriptural, bona fide Church. It is a question that everyone must answer.

*He said to them, "But who do you say that I am?" Simon Peter answered and said, "You are the Christ, the Son of the living God." Jesus answered and said to him, "Blessed are you, Simon Bar-Jonah, for flesh and blood has not revealed this to you, but My Father who is in heaven. And I also say to you that you are Peter, and on this rock I will build My church, and the gates of Hades shall not prevail against it" (Matthew 16:15-18 NKJV).*

Jesus promised that He would "*build*" the Church,

and Peter was included in the very first, integral part of founding that construction. The development and growth of that spiritual Church "building" continues to be built upon with multitudes of believers to this very day.

*Now, therefore, you are no longer strangers and foreigners, but fellow citizens with the saints and members of the household of God, having been built on the foundation of the apostles and prophets, Jesus Christ Himself being the chief corner stone, in whom the whole building, being joined together, grows into a holy temple in the Lord (Ephesians 2:19-21 NKJV).*

Clearly, the Lord is the builder. The Word shows us that, unless the Lord builds the house, one's labor is useless.[10] Our foundation and roots are in Him. Furthermore, only Jesus saves—not pastors, evangelists, missionaries, nor any other people. Flesh and blood are not able to birth a Christian. Spiritual rooting that enacts Salvation and builds the Church is divine.

*Humans can reproduce only human life, but the Holy Spirit gives birth to spiritual life (John 3:6 NLT).*

God wants to use you mightily (like He did Peter, the other apostles, and the early Christians) in order to lead people to Himself, so that the Church will continue to be built.[11] Still, our efforts are futile without the Spirit of God. The apostle Paul prayed for God to give people a spirit of wisdom and of revelation so that they could know God.[12] Then, He can use us.

*Let your roots grow down into him, and let your lives be built on him. Then your faith will grow strong in the truth you were taught, and you will overflow with thankfulness (Colossians 2:7 NLT).*

When the Church began, they didn't have pews,

5

stained-glass windows, sound systems, overhead screens, or any of the other paraphernalia we find in churches nowadays. Don't misunderstand me, those things are nice for us to have, and they provide many benefits. Nevertheless, from the beginning, the core of success for the early believers was that they were continually meeting together.

*Every day they continued to meet together in the temple courts. They broke bread in their homes and ate together with glad and sincere hearts, praising God and enjoying the favor of all the people. And the Lord added to their number daily those who were being saved (Acts 2:46-47 NIV).*

It's natural for those who share common interests to want to be together. It might be job-related, a hobby, a love of sports, music, food, or various other pursuits. Those of us who love God especially want to be with each other, because we are rooted together.

*They will be like a tree planted by the water that sends out its roots by the stream. It does not fear when heat comes; its leaves are always green. It has no worries in a year of drought and never fails to bear fruit (Jeremiah 17:8 NIV).*

# CULTIVATING QUESTIONS

### For Chapter 1

1. Describe the difference between the Church and the church building where we go to worship.

2. At what event was the Holy Spirit first given to the Church?

3. Share something that you may know about your family's roots and ancestry.

4. Read Ephesians 3:17-19. How are Christians rooted together?

5. What are some things which keep the roots of plants from thriving? (See Luke 8:14)

6. What makes the branches holy, and how can we be built up and strengthened? (See Romans 11:16 and Colossians 2:6-7.)

7. Read Proverbs 12:3. What guarantees secure rooting?

# Chapter 2

# GRAFTING

*There is neither Jew nor Greek, there is neither slave nor free man, there is neither male nor female; for you are all one in Christ Jesus (Galatians 3:28 NASB).*

In horticultural and agricultural trades, grafting is a commonly used technique that joins a cutting from one plant to another already growing plant so they can grow together and propagate. With this method, a shoot of the desired plant, once grafted into the existing plant, is encouraged to grow by pruning off the stem of the existing plant just above the newly grafted bud.

Read the eleventh chapter of Romans to see how other nations were "grafted" into the family of God's chosen people. There we learn that God's gift of life, blessing and preference also came to the Gentiles (i.e., any person who is not an Israelite). The Bible tells us that this wonderful mystery of salvation became available to people everywhere in the world, because the people of Israel had hardened their hearts and rejected Jesus Christ as their Messiah.

*Again I ask: Did they stumble so as to fall beyond recovery?*

*Not at all! Rather, because of their transgression, salvation has come to the Gentiles to make Israel envious. But if their transgression means riches for the world, and their loss means riches for the Gentiles, how much greater riches will their full inclusion bring (Romans 11:11-12 NIV).*

All people who receive Christ as their Savior are divinely grafted into the original branches by the mercy and grace of God, and thus share this regal affiliation that was first offered to God's chosen people.

*Do not boast against the branches. But if you do boast, remember that you do not support the root, but the root supports you. You will say then, "Branches were broken off that I might be grafted in." Well said. Because of unbelief they were broken off, and you stand by faith. Do not be haughty, but fear. For if God did not spare the natural branches, He may not spare you either (Romans 11:18-21 NKJV).*

In Lamentation 3:40 we read, *"Let us test and examine our ways."* There is no place for superiority or inferiority in Christ, but we are told to simply remain in His love.[13] To remain means to continue. Abiding in Jesus is the only way to have life.

The tremendous privileges that we obtain through this holy grafting shouldn't be taken for granted. A graft gets life and strength from the plant that it's grafted into, and we are grafted into God's very distinguished family. Because of this consecration, we are linked to the marvelous promises that He has given to His chosen people, some of which were given many years before Jesus was born.

*Through Christ Jesus, God has blessed the Gentiles with the same blessing he promised to Abraham, so that we who are* believers might receive the promised Holy Spirit through faith *(Galatians 3:14 NLT)*.

God said that through Abraham, all the nations of the earth would be blessed,[14] and since the beginning of time as we know it, God has had a plan for everyone. His intention was that mankind would be saved and receive His mercy and grace, which ultimately came through the sacrifice of His Son, Jesus Christ.

*And if you belong to Christ, then you are Abraham's descendants, heirs according to promise (Galatians 3:29 NASB).*

We've heard about beneficiaries who've inherited millions of dollars from extremely wealthy people who died, or those who received phenomenal incomes from their celebrity parents or spouses. Like me, perhaps you've wondered how it would feel to have great monetary wealth. Maybe you've speculated about how it would feel to win the lottery. Our Heavenly Father's generosity to us far exceeds any worldly treasure, and those who have submitted their lives to Jesus Christ have an inheritance that is beyond description.

*But as it is written: "Eye has not seen, nor ear heard, Nor have entered into the heart of man The things which God has prepared for those who love Him" (1 Corinthians 2:9 NKJV).*

The Pharisees didn't believe that Gentiles should have entitlement to the promises given to their ancestors through the patriarchs and prophets. Apparently, they didn't see God as a God of equality.[15] Instead of depending on His Grace, they trusted in their works and the Jewish laws, not realizing that love and faith are the epitome of life.[16]

Although some of the Jews finally came around to the

truth, it took a lot of convincing before they could accept it. Peter's words recorded in the book of Acts brought a change of heart to many of them.

*When the others heard this, they stopped objecting and began praising God. They said, "We can see that God has also given the Gentiles the privilege of repenting of their sins and receiving eternal life" (Acts 11:18 NLT).*

Prophets foretold the impartial redemption of *all* people that would be done in God's perfect timing. However, when the time had come for Christ to be revealed, so many people missed it. Their Savior was right in front of them, and they didn't know it.

*What then? What the people of Israel sought so earnestly they did not obtain. The elect among them did, but the others were hardened, as it is written: "God gave them a spirit of stupor, eyes that could not see and ears that could not hear, to this very day" (Romans 11:7-8 NIV).*

Some of us have said with perplexity, "God works in mysterious ways." Although that statement can't be found in the Bible, God did tell us that His thoughts and ways are very different from ours.[17] The essence of all divine timing pertains to His marvelous purposes, which we cannot expect to understand completely.

The grafting couldn't happen until all the important particulars were in place. Often, we are blind to the reasons for delays in those seemingly urgent things we feel should be accomplished quickly. Jesus told His disciples that it wasn't for them to know God's timing.[18] Not even the angels know all of God's timing (including when Christ will be returning).[19]

Jesus said, ". . . *my father is the Gardener.*"[20] An

experienced gardener knows that the best time for grafting certain kinds of vines is usually done some time in late summer, when buds are fully developed. Other types of grafting might do better if done in the spring. Farmers and agriculturists know that if they can figure out the perfect timing of grafting, it will produce the best plants, but God always has perfect timing.

*But when the fullness of the time had come, God sent forth His Son, born of a woman, born under the law, to redeem those who were under the law, that we might receive the adoption as sons (Galatians 4:4-5 NKJV).*

The Gentile's grafting into God's chosen was made possible through Jesus Christ, so that all those who have faith in Him would be considered children of Abraham. This was God's powerful plan from the beginning, and it is His will that *all* people, not just the Jews, become His children.[21]

*As the Scriptures tell us, "Anyone who trusts in him will never be disgraced." Jew and Gentile are the same in this respect. They have the same Lord, who gives generously to all who call on him. For "Everyone who calls on the name of the LORD will be saved" (Romans 10:11-13 NLT).*

# CULTIVATING QUESTIONS

## For Chapter 2

1.  According to Romans 11:25, how long will the people of Israel have hard hearts or blindness regarding salvation through Jesus Christ?

2.  What person did the Lord tell Ananias that He would use to proclaim His name to the Gentiles? (See Acts 9:11-15.)

3.  According to Paul, in Romans 3:9, how are Jews and Gentiles alike?

4.  Who is described in Isaiah 42:1-4 as the one who will bring justice to all people?

5.  What is the inheritance mentioned in Ephesians 1:18?

6.  Read Matthew 24:44. Why did Jesus tell His disciples to ". . . *be ready*," and what timing was He speaking about?

7.  According to Galatians 3:7, who are the children of Abraham?

*Chapter 3*

# DENOMINATIONS

*For as the body is one and has many members, but all the members of that one body, being many, are one body, so also is Christ. For by one Spirit we were all baptized into one body—whether Jews or Greeks, whether slaves or free—and have all been made to drink into one Spirit (1 Corinthians 12:12-13 NKJV).*

Although there are other kinds of fruits that grow on vines, grapes are the fruit that is often used as a symbol in Christianity. There are examples in Hosea 9:10 and Isaiah 5:1-7, which compare Israel to a vineyard of grapes. Perhaps God's people were described this way because grapes had relative value culturally, and grapes were very familiar to the people in those Biblical times.

Today, there are over 10,000 different varieties of grapes in the world. As I was thinking about this, I also began to think about the diversity in cultures, in people, and particularly, all the differences in religions, including the plethora of Christian denominations.

Although it's impossible to know exactly how many religions there are, it is estimated to be over four thousand different ones. Yet, just because they have been defined as a religion doesn't mean they are correct in their teachings. Deplorably, there are many counterfeits which lead people astray.

One simplified definition of religion is: "A belief in a divine or superhuman power or powers to be obeyed and worshiped as the creator(s) and ruler(s) of any specific system of belief and worship, often involving a code of ethics and a philosophy."[22]

According to that definition, it would be rather easy to create a religion that has nothing to do with the Word of God, and we know there are many religions that do not have anything to do with the Bible. Jesus warned His disciples of those people which spread delusion and aberrant beliefs.[23] We need to watch out for fakes.

*But these speak evil of whatever they do not know; and whatever they know naturally, like brute beasts, in these things they corrupt themselves (Jude 1:10 NKJV).*

Sometimes religious people are selective in what they teach from the Bible and dangerously ignore what they don't want to hear. We need to ask ourselves, even if the truth hurts, wouldn't it be better than believing a lie and remaining in darkness? When we walk in the dark, we're sure to stumble.

*For the time will come when they will not endure sound doctrine; but wanting to have their ears tickled, they will accumulate for themselves teachers in accordance to their own desires, and will turn away their ears from the truth and will turn aside to myths (2 Timothy 4:3-4 NASB).*

False religions can be examined and proved wrong in the light of the Holy Scriptures. Examples that quickly reveal erroneous religions are seen in those that fail to teach that salvation is obtainable through the Blood of Jesus Christ and His sacrificial death on the Cross. Also, any religion that teaches that one can be good enough in order to earn forgiveness, or that Jesus was only a mere man and not God, do not teach the truth.

There are thousands of strange, counterfeit beliefs in the myriad of cults, superstitions, humanistic philosophies and satanic beliefs. I won't dwell on this extensive subject. However, there are many books available by Christian authors that explain various heresies, if you want to learn more. Meanwhile, the best definitions of true religion are found in the Bible.

*Pure and undefiled religion before God and the Father is this: to visit orphans and widows in their trouble, and to keep oneself unspotted from the world (James 1:27 NKJV).*

I regret that sometimes we may make Christianity a subject that we try to define only by our denomination. We may be convinced that our choice of a church is the only right one, but any attempt to put the Church in a denominational "box" doesn't work. Our dogmatic opinions can cause division instead of unity among our brothers and sisters and harm those who may be seeking the truth.

I believe that one reason God has allowed more than one denomination for the Church is because our human perspective and assertions are very narrow compared to the magnitude of truth. God's thoughts and ways are beyond our complete comprehension.[24] Can we all admit that our individual stances are simply never enough in grasping all theology?

Although different evangelical denominations include

doctrinal basics of the Gospel that we can easily agree upon, maybe you've noticed that each church largely seems to emphasize and focus on specific Scriptural teaching. Interestingly, we often find that this concentration of a denomination identifies the fellowship. As we look at the distinctive messages accentuated in a theme, such as baptism, spiritual gifts, holiness, worship, grace, faith and sanctification, we might form conclusions about whether they are Baptist, Lutheran, Methodist, Pentecostal, etc.

Another likely reason for why there are so many denominations is because, like our physical body, the Body of Christ has many parts, and not every part has the exact same need or preference. The following verse speaks of our diversity.

*For in fact the body is not one member but many. If the foot should say, "Because I am not a hand, I am not of the body," is it therefore not of the body? And if the ear should say, "Because I am not an eye, I am not of the body," is it therefore not of the body? If the whole body were an eye, where would be the hearing? If the whole were hearing, where would be the smelling? But now God has set the members, each one of them, in the body just as He pleased. And if they were all one member, where would the body be? But now indeed there are many members, yet one body (1 Corinthians 12:14-20 NKJV).*

Although we may likely be drawn to those with similar beliefs and preferences, Christians are not like cookie cutter images. We are wonderfully, uniquely different, and finding the place in the church that the Lord has in mind for us is very significant to our life and health. Pray that God will show you exactly where you need to be, and He will surely direct you.

*Since you are my rock and my fortress, for the sake of your name lead and guide me (Psalm 31:3 NIV).*

The fourteenth chapter of Romans elaborates on various types of beliefs among the early Christians, and it was clear that all those believers didn't agree on everything. The apostle Paul warned them to be careful so that they wouldn't cause a brother to stumble because of foolish controversies. Just because we don't agree on everything, doesn't mean we can't be one in the love of Jesus.

Although there is diversity in the Body of Christ, we must do our best to keep unity,[25] despite our differences. Time-honored doctrines and theologies are important, and they have their place, but denominational tradition mustn't be the major component for any church.

Tony Evans wrote, "Satan wants to split the family of God because he understands something that many Christians do not: God's work and involvement is greatly reduced in a context of disunity."[26] Jesus stressed the importance of love,[27] and any creed or persuasion that disallows this foremost consideration should be abandoned.

*But solid food is for the mature, who by constant use have trained themselves to distinguish good from evil (Hebrews 5:14 NIV).*

As we draw nearer to the day of Christ's return, it appears that the various branches of our traditional churches are proclaiming broader and more inclusive expressions of sound doctrine and Biblical principles, rather than merely elaborating on the portion which was once their main voicing. Although sectarianism has purpose, just as structures have walls for a reason, again, our goal should be to eliminate any estrangement between our brothers and sisters, so that no denominational wall will cause discord.

We will all thrive if we are willing to change and grow, certainly not to match the world, but to bring revival with the good news of the Gospel. As Christians from all churches join forces and connect in love, without prejudice or diluting the truth, we gain strength. This ideal has been compared to the powerful source made when small, individual streams trickling through the land meet to form a mighty rushing river. That power can move mountains!

*Now these are the gifts Christ gave to the church: the apostles, the prophets, the evangelists, and the pastors and teachers. Their responsibility is to equip God's people to do his work and build up the church, the body of Christ. This will continue until we all come to such unity in our faith and knowledge of God's Son that we will be mature in the Lord, measuring up to the full and complete standard of Christ (Ephesians 4:11-13 NLT).*

# CULTIVATING QUESTIONS

## For Chapter 3

1. Do you recognize the denominational emphasis of your home church? If so, what is it?

2. Name one thing that you think should be especially emphasized in all Christian denominations.

3. Read Acts 9:31. As indicated in this verse, what helps churches to grow?

4. What is something that would indicate a false religion?

5. What did Jesus say were the most important commandments? (See Mark 12:29-31)

6. Write what you think the following verse means in your own words: *There are differences of ministries, but the same Lord. And there are diversities of activities, but it is the same God who works all in all (1 Corinthians 12:5-6 NKJV).*

7.  1 Corinthians 12:25-26 describes the empathy we
    need to have for our brothers and sisters in the Lord.
    Give an example of how your church might show
    support to another ministry.

*Chapter 4*

# PLANTING

*". . . But he who received seed on the good ground is he who hears the word and understands it, who indeed bears fruit and produces: some a hundredfold, some sixty, some thirty" (Matthew 13:23 NKJV).*

The other day, I noticed a beautiful plant with bright red flowers in the backyard of a friend's home. I was given a clipping off the plant after I mentioned how lovely it was, but absentmindedly, I forgot about it and left it in my car after I drove back home. Then, a few days later, I found the clipping wilted and dead, because I hadn't given it water and put it into the soil as needed.

This incident with the plant clipping reminded me of some people who have failed to find their place in the church. It's sad for me to watch them weakening spiritually, because church attendance is no longer a priority in their lives. They claim to be Christians, but they've been distracted with other matters.

It is so important for everyone to be planted in the good soil of a church, and it is imperative to life and growth. Without it, we begin to wilt, and we won't survive for very long. Everyone is dangerously more vulnerable to the elements when not receiving the vital nutrients which are available in a congregation among believers.

The Bible teaches us that people who delight in the law of the Lord can be compared to trees that are planted beside the water: their leaves never wither.[28] Being planted in good soil is a matter of spiritual health, and, for some, it could be a matter of life and death. We war against the principalities and powers of darkness that literally want to destroy our life in Jesus.[29] We need all the information and help we can get to withstand our demonic enemies, and we can find that help through the ministry of the Church.

*His intent was that now,* **through the church,** *the manifold wisdom of God should be made known to the rulers and authorities in the heavenly realms, according to his eternal purpose that he accomplished in Christ Jesus our Lord (Ephesians 3:10-11 NIV; emphasis added).*

Because you are reading this book, it is likely that you have already been planted in a church home. Nevertheless, whether you've already found your place or not, it is also possible, for one reason or another, that there will come a day when you might need to be planted in another church. Perhaps you are looking for your place to be with other believers right now.

Again, I emphasize my belief that Christians can be strengthened and empowered by meeting together regularly with their brothers and sisters in Christ. The following verse is a reminder of that consideration.

*Let us think of ways to motivate one another to acts of love and good works. And let us not neglect our meeting together, as some people do, but encourage one another, especially now that the day of his return is drawing near (Hebrews 10:24-25 NLT).*

Have you ever considered that the only place that we can function effectively is within the Church? We will not function well without each other. The apostle Paul shows why this is true by comparing the Church to a human body.

*If the foot should say, "Because I am not a hand, I am not of the body," is it therefore not of the body? And if the ear should say, "Because I am not an eye, I am not of the body," is it therefore not of the body? If the whole body were an eye, where would be the hearing? If the whole were hearing, where would be the smelling? (1 Corinthians 12:15-17 NKJV).*

Obviously, the human body has physical parts needed for life and functioning. To mention a few necessities, we need our lungs to breathe, our liver to filter impurities and our brains for thinking. The Body of Christ has spiritual parts that are also indispensable and work together for life and functioning, and because of that fact, each of us needs to have that place where we can grow and move healthfully, rooted and grounded in the church.

We may not see it clearly, yet, however infinitesimally, plants and all living things are changing and growing all the time. If there isn't change and growth, and the plant's needs are not supplied, it will shrivel up and die like the little plant clipping that I forgot in my car. Once it was dead, it couldn't be revived, and although I tried, it was too late. There are similarities in our spiritual lives. When we aren't planted, we are in great danger of wilting and drying up.

*I pray that out of his glorious riches he may strengthen you with power through his Spirit in your inner being, so that Christ may dwell in your hearts through faith. And I pray that you, being rooted and established in love, may have power, together with all the Lord's holy people, to grasp how wide and long and high and deep is the love of Christ. . . (Ephesians 3:16-18 NIV).*

The words that stand out to me in that verse are *"together with all the Lord's holy people."* I think in this letter, Paul wanted converts to know the significance of being *"together"* in order to experience God's power and comprehend the love of Jesus.

Years ago, John Donne, a powerful writer and preacher, wrote the famous phrase that you've probably heard, "No man is an island." His words expressed the idea that human beings do badly when isolated from others—and we need each other in order to thrive.

*If one person falls, the other can reach out and help. But someone who falls alone is in real trouble (Ecclesiastes 4:10 NLT).*

We can see that many people in this world are lonely. Studies have indicated that a person with perpetual loneliness will eventually be more susceptible to severe depression and dementia. Those awful feelings of loneliness can happen to those who have no friends or family and those who feel as if they don't have anywhere to belong. Even the Psalmist expressed that he was as "lonely as a solitary bird on the roof."[30] However, he learned where to find comfort.

*A father of the fatherless and a judge for the widows, Is God in His holy habitation. God makes a home for the lonely; He leads out the prisoners into prosperity, Only the rebellious dwell in a parched land (Psalm 68:5-6 NASB).*

One man wisely said, "When I feel truly alone, with a sense of being lost, even empty inside, it is then that I realize I have unknowingly moved away from God, so I move back." I suppose that everyone has experienced loneliness at one time or another. Nevertheless, loneliness has a remedy. Finding a caring church home will help alleviate loneliness.

Now that we've looked at this important premise of being planted, let's consider a few things to look for in order to find the rightful place where we can be planted. Because there are many denominations (as noted in chapter 3), careful examination of a church's doctrine and beliefs is central to the choice of a church. Sound teaching is a most important consideration. Most churches have a doctrinal statement that can be reviewed before a decision is made. The doctrine should represent what the Bible teaches without compromise, additions or detractions.

Other considerations to look for include: Is this a praying church? When you attend a service, can you sense that the Holy Spirit is leading the service? Do you feel welcome and experience God's love through the pastor and the members of the church? Is grace through faith emphasized? Do the ministries of the church accommodate your age group or that of the members of your family? Is the sermon applicable to your everyday life and growth? Is the music uplifting? Are you encouraged to worship? Is the church location convenient or near enough to your neighborhood?

There are no perfect people or perfect churches, but you still might make a checklist and attempt to define those things which are important to you in a church. Most importantly, ask God to lead you to the place where *He* wants you to be, because that is where you'll grow and be most fulfilled. Also, keep in mind that it isn't all about what the church can give to you, but it includes what you can do to help build the church.

*And this I pray, that your love may abound still more and more in knowledge and all discernment, that you may approve the things that are excellent, that you may be sincere and without offense till the day of Christ, being filled with the fruits of righteousness which are by Jesus Christ, to the glory and praise of God (Philippians 1:9-11 NKJV).*

# CULTIVATING QUESTIONS

### For Chapter 4

1.  Ecclesiastes 3:2 indicates that there is *"A time to plant."* Are you now, or have you ever been, well-planted in a church? (Keep in mind that being well planted isn't a matter of months or years.)

2.  Who makes us grow? (See 1 Corinthians 3:6-7.)

3.  What benefits are described in Jeremiah 17:7-8 for those who trust in the Lord?

4.  Read Job 8:11-13. What do these verses say will happen to plants that don't receive sustenance?

5.  Name at least two or more things that are important to you in your choice of a church home?

6.  Give a reason why is it helpful for you to join forces with other Christians, rather than remaining isolated without fellowship with believers? (See Ecclesiastes 4:12.)

7. There are many who are called to be leaders in the church, but who is the Head of everything for the Church, as seen in Ephesians 1:22–23?

# Chapter 5

# FERTILIZER

*I will sing for the one I love a song about his vineyard: My loved one had a vineyard on a fertile hillside (Isaiah 5:1 NIV).*

If the ground is fertile, it means that plants will produce abundantly, because the ground is rich in resources which produce favorable results. Farmers put fertilizer in the soil to improve both the quality and the quantity of crop growth and production, and agriculturists understand that fertilizer is essential for the world's crops to be healthy. Food production and crop yields would be significantly reduced if the nutrients that crops remove from the soil were not replaced.

Just as plants need fertilizer for maximum production, humans also have nutritional needs that require regular attention and replacement. Although our culture seems to place more priority upon physical needs, meeting our need for our spiritual nutrient requirements is much more important. Jesus made this clear to us when He was tested by the devil in the wilderness. After fasting for forty days and nights, He was unimaginably hungry and thirsty when the tempter suggested that He turn stones into bread.

*But He answered and said, "It is written, 'Man shall not live by bread alone, but by every word that proceeds from the mouth of God'" (Matthew 4:4 NKJV).*

God's Word is essential for vibrant life and health. Sleep, exercise and healthy food and drink aren't the only means of restoration for human beings. The apostle Paul indicated that bodily discipline has only a little profit, but godliness is profitable for now and forever.[31]

There's something else that can supply us with vitality, and it's free! (Maybe I should say, it's *still* free.) Again, I refer to what is available in our churches. It's where we assemble with other believers and where we can give and receive encouragement and strength.

*The righteous shall flourish like a palm tree, He shall grow like a cedar in Lebanon. Those who are planted in the house of the LORD Shall flourish in the courts of our God (Psalm 92:12-13 NKJV).*

In many parts of the globe, people don't have the freedom to attend church. In some countries, public preaching and gatherings of the church are forbidden, and Bibles aren't allowed. Those of us who live where we are free to attend church, fellowship with other believers and have easy access to our Bibles may forget what a great privilege it is to have these opportunities.

*Bless the LORD, O my soul, And forget not all His benefits (Psalm 103:2 NKJV).*

The amassing of provisions for our physical needs alone, whether housing, food, clothes, entertainment, etc., often rises in priority and consideration over the provision for our spiritual needs. However, whether spiritual needs are provided or not has a much greater impact upon one's life. Those things that are seen with our eyes should not be elevated in importance above what is unseen.

*There's far more here than meets the eye. The things we see now are here today, gone tomorrow. But the things we can't see now will last forever (2 Corinthians 4:18 MSG).*

Like farmers using fertilizer to maintain the level of nutrients in soils, we need to get the balance right, keeping in mind that our greatest need is not physical but spiritual. Along with Bible study and prayer, a great portion of our spiritual needs can be met through the local church. To be healthy branches, we need the "fertilizer" given to us through the teaching of the Word, which will help us grow fruit.[32] God purposely placed pastors, teachers, and evangelists in the Church to help us be productive.

*Be responsive to your pastoral leaders. Listen to their counsel. They are alert to the condition of your lives and work under the strict supervision of God. Contribute to the joy of their leadership, not its drudgery. Why would you want to make things harder for them? (Hebrews 13:17 MSG).*

It has been difficult for many of our pastors to watch their congregations declining in numbers during the pandemic, and it has been no easy task for them to convince people to return when things improved. Unfortunately, attendance records continue to show lower numbers. People quickly became accustomed to sleeping in on Sunday mornings, rationalizing that virtual services are their alternative. However, it's apparent that the numbers of people watching online church has also taken a dive. The lifestyle of a lot of once faithful church goers has been tragically changed.

Dr. Phil McGraw advised, "It is an undeniable truth that one year from now your life will be better or it will be worse, but it won't be the same."[33] In America, we can make our lives better by choosing to grow and learn, and valuable Biblical instruction is available to us through church attendance.

We should be working as farmers who remember the processes that are helpful for optimal production. Like plants that need fertilizer to thrive, every believer needs nourishment for life. God has blessed our churches, and it is He who supplies essential needs through them for His children. Jesus told us we can do nothing on our own, apart from Him.[34]

The Dead Sea, which is located on the border between Israel and Jordan, can be compared to people who don't get the balance right in their lives. It is a salt-filled lake that is almost six times as salty as the ocean, and it is devoid of life. No river outlet originates from the sea, so nothing lives in it.

Religious people who won't go to church, or those who go to church but never get involved, may have collected a lot of Scripture in their minds, but they don't produce fruit or really live the truth. You could say they are devoid of life, like the Dead Sea. Maybe they have accumulated a lot of "salt" or "fertilizer," but they have no outlet and are not useful. Christianity isn't about just knowing truths from the Bible. Even the devil knows the Word.[35]

I think of Jim Elliot, a famous missionary to the Auca Indians in Ecuador, and what he said when he was asked why he was so determined to go to a foreign country to teach God's Word instead of the United States. He responded, "What if the well-filled church in the homeland needs stirring? They have the Scriptures, Moses and the prophets, and a whole lot more. Their condemnation is written on their bank books and in the dust of their Bible covers."[36]

It is possible to know the truth and even attend church regularly and still not be nourished or share nourishment. Each of us has a responsibility to keep ourselves healthy in body, soul and spirit, and to be alert to the needs of others. The key to taking care of nutritional needs is through being rooted and grounded in God's fertile vineyard.

*Blessed are those who hunger and thirst for righteousness, for they shall be satisfied (Matthew 5:6 NASB).*

The words that come out of our mouths will reflect whether we truly desire to give and receive nourishment or not. Words can be like poison that will rot a plant, or, words can be like fertilizer that brings healthy growth and life. The book of Proverbs teaches us many lessons about what words can do. The following verse is only one example.

*The tongue has the power of life and death, and those who love it will eat its fruit (Proverbs 18:21 NIV).*

There is no life without Jesus. God sent His Son that we might live through Him.[37] That is how we can live and thrive, and since we are the Body of Christ, we need each other in order to glow with health and vitality.

*You take care of the earth and water it, making it rich and fertile. The river of God has plenty of water; it provides a bountiful harvest of grain, for you have ordered it so. You drench the plowed ground with rain, melting the clods and leveling the ridges. You soften the earth with showers and bless its abundant crops. You crown the year with a bountiful harvest; even the hard pathways overflow with abundance (Psalm 65:9-11 NLT).*

# CULTIVATING QUESTIONS

## For Chapter 5

1. What do you think is the milk which will bring growth as noted in 1 Peter 2:2-3?

2. Read John 15:4-8, and then write in a few words what abiding in Jesus means to you.

3. Name at least one resource that a good church can provide to keep you spiritually healthy.

4. On a scale of 1 to 10, rate how spiritually nourished you've been this week (1 being depleted or starving, and 10 being completely satisfied).

5. Our physical needs are important, but why is the condition of our souls more significant to our health? (See 3 John 1:2.)

6. How is every need for healthy life and growth supplied? (See Philippians 4:19.)

7. How could your spiritual imbalance affect the Body of Christ? (See 1 Corinthians 12:26.)

*Chapter 6*

# WATERING

*He covers the sky with clouds; he supplies the earth with rain and makes grass grow on the hills (Psalm 147:8 NIV).*

The primary source of freshwater for the world is rain. Water is necessary for our survival, and all living things depend on water to live. Our human bodies are made up of 60-70% water. For our organs to work properly, we need to be well-hydrated. Although we may survive a month without food, it is unlikely that we could survive much longer than three days without water. In comparison, we also can't subsist spiritually without what Jesus called "living water."

You may remember the Biblical story about the Samaritan woman who met Jesus at the well when she came to draw water from it. Jesus shared some crucial information with her, and her life was dramatically changed.

*Jesus replied, "If you only knew the gift God has for you and who you are speaking to, you would ask me, and I would give you living water" (John 4:10 NLT).*

Those words are for you and me also. Just like the

Samaritan woman, we can ask Jesus to give us that water. After hearing what Jesus told her, she went into town and shared what she heard, and many other Samaritans believed because of her testimony. Surely, that living water brought life to her and her acquaintances, and it can do the same for everyone. However, when people isolate themselves from Christian fellowship, there is less occasion to share and receive it.

I like to think that, because God is love,[38] the essence of the living water which is found through the Word is the love of God. We learn to give and receive His love in community where we can be "watered," and our churches are an obvious place to supply that refreshing "irrigation."

*There is a river whose streams make glad the city of God, The holy dwelling places of the Most High (Psalm 46:4 NASB).*

Separation from the dwelling places of God is dehydrating. Satan will attempt to disconnect people, because separation makes people vulnerable to the misery of loneliness and lovelessness. We will literally dry up and die if we don't interact in love. Jesus' command for us to love one another was for our own good.

Some people may unconsciously see love as kind of an idealistic or religious attitude, but living without it means death. Perhaps it is a slow death in those who have become carelessly complacent about activating love, but love has miraculous, life–giving power when it's initiated.

*Dear friends, since God so loved us, we also ought to love one another. No one has ever seen God; but if we love one another, God lives in us and his love is made complete in us (1 John 4:11-12 NIV).*

The verse in the preceding paragraph shows us that *if*

we love one another, God lives in us. On the other hand, if we don't love one another, we are incomplete and not abiding in Him.

Admittedly, the Holy Spirit has convicted me many times when I have allowed my mind to think ugly, hateful thoughts. No, I'm not perfect, and if you're honest, I'm sure you could also admit you've had those kinds of wicked thoughts. When we entertain the devil's lies, we make ourselves susceptible to dehydration. I've learned that judgmental or unloving responses to people are always unacceptable to God, no matter what the provocation. Hate is a ploy of Satan to ruin us, and Jesus warned of the severe consequences of responding with anger and hatred.

*But I say, if you are even angry with someone, you are subject to judgment! If you call someone an idiot, you are in danger of being brought before the court. And if you curse someone, you are in danger of the fires of hell (Matthew 5:22 NLT).*

Love, like water, is basic and necessary for growth and life. We can't live without it. We were created to love, and that is our most important purpose. So, we must make every effort to give the love of God by the act of our will.

*Therefore, as we have opportunity, let us do good to all people, especially to those who belong to the family of believers (Galatians 6:10 NIV).*

Everyone who loves God, will love His children also.[39] Those who purposely avoid church attendance are not showing much love to those in the household of faith. God wants us to love, not only those we may be drawn to naturally but even those we may not necessarily want to be around. We are to love even those we may consider undeserving, and those who may cause us pain.

The bottom line is that we have been commanded to love, and interestingly, as we choose to love, looking past whatever conflict, we grow in health and maturity.

*Jesus replied, "You must love the LORD your God with all your heart, all your soul, and all your mind.' This is the first and greatest commandment. A second is equally important: 'Love your neighbor as yourself'" (Matthew 22:37-39 NLT).*

Just as water supplies a basic need, love nourishes and produces beauty and growth. Yes, love will make you beautiful. However, unlike drinking water, the living water of love helps to keep us personally attractive and healthy, vitalizes the body, soul and spirit, and it also brings refreshment to those around us.

*"He who believes in Me, as the Scripture has said, out of his heart will flow rivers of living water" (John 7:38 NKJV).*

There is a church in the area where I live which is named "The Well." I like that name, because it implies a spiritual reservoir where people can go to be replenished, benefitting body, soul and spirit—and that is what a church is supposed to do. I know some of the members of this congregation, and they place a high value on church attendance, experiencing the joy of oneness with other believers at this house of worship.

*How good and pleasant it is when God's people live together in unity! It is like precious oil poured on the head, running down on the beard, running down on Aaron's beard, down on the collar of his robe (Psalm 133:1-2 NIV).*

There still seems to be a lot of people who, previously, were regular church attendees but have come to prefer virtual church services. I think this preference was mostly developed during the pandemic. Beyond the precautionary safety issues which were instilled throughout the world to avoid close contact, it became kind of convenient not to have to get dressed, drive anywhere, and meet early schedules. The trouble with that is, among other things, virtual services don't remove the thirst that comes from loneliness and the need for human contact.

Virtual church services are a blessing to those who have disabilities that prohibit leaving their home, but demonstrative affection, such as hugs, handshakes and encouraging pats on the back, can't be supplied electronically. A virtual glass filled with water doesn't quench one's thirst.

It's harder to express intimacy and caring through a video alone. People who love each other need human contact, and psychologists tell us that touch is one of the most basic, primal needs.

We see instances throughout the Bible where Jesus and the disciples used touch by the laying on of hands in demonstration of love and healing. Loving touch can be used as a cure to combat sickness, loneliness and hatred, and it is a natural way for humans to respond to one another. Sometimes touch speaks louder than words. It helps us to trust and bond with one another. Also, there is scientific proof that touch is beneficial to our immune system, decreasing health problems. The fact is, we need physical contact as much as we need water, and the church supplies this, yet another survival need to the community.

*Let us acknowledge the L*ORD*; let us press on to acknowledge him. As surely as the sun rises, he will appear; he will come to us like the winter rains, like the spring rains that water the earth (Hosea 6:3 NIV)*

# CULTIVATING QUESTIONS

## For Chapter 6

1. Read Job 8:11–13 and tell how this passage can be related to our need for the *"Living water"* that Jesus offered to the Samaritan woman.

2. To what drink is 1 Corinthians 12:13 referring?

3. What was the gift that Jesus was talking about in John 4:10? (Also see Revelation 21:6.)

4. Where does living water flow from in a born-again Christian? (See John 7:38.)

5. Name some ways that your spiritual thirst can be satisfied.

6. Do you think the practice of "laying on of hands" is important? If so, why?

Chapter 7

# PRUNING

*I am the Real Vine and my Father is the Farmer. He cuts off every branch of me that doesn't bear grapes. And every branch that is grape-bearing he prunes back so it will bear even more (John 15:2 MSG).*

I'm told by a farmer friend, that producing his delicious, succulent grapes takes him about two years, and during that period, pruning is very necessary. Dead wood must be removed, along with foliage that has little fruit. Even if the foliage *appears* healthy, if the buds don't have sufficient sunlight, grapes will not grow well. So, he must thin the foliage to produce as much fruit as possible.

Using symbolism, Jesus explained that He is the Vine and we are the branches. His Father, the Vinedresser (Gardener/Farmer), will prune the branches so that we will bear more fruit. The apostle Paul tells us about the fruit in Galatians 5:22-23. We will look at this more closely in chapter 9.

Fruitfulness is the goal of pruning. It may sound harsh, but, clearly, Christians are either fruitful or they are not really Christians. If the branch does not bear fruit, it's dead, and it's cut off. Jesus spoke of the awful destination of hypocrites who don't produce good fruit.[40] Even though some may profess to be a disciple and appear healthy, they are not true followers if there is no fruit. However, those who have received Jesus Christ as Savior and Lord will indeed bear fruit—and they will surely be pruned. In Scripture, we are told about different things which need to be eliminated (or I could say pruned) from the branches. Bitterness is one example.

*Looking carefully lest anyone fall short of the grace of God; lest any root of bitterness springing up cause trouble, and by this many become defiled (Hebrews 12:15 NKJV).*

Our Father prunes us in order to remove things from our lives that hinder us from fruitfulness—but that doesn't mean we're going to enjoy the process. In fact, it may be quite painful. Nevertheless, pruning isn't meant to harm us but rather to improve us. He wants to prune away meaningless, distracting things which weigh us down and keep us from a rich and satisfying life that He wants us to have. Every cut is for our good.

*The thief does not come except to steal, and to kill, and to destroy. I have come that they may have life, and that they may have it more abundantly (John 10:9-10 NKJV).*

Some examples of what might need pruning could be unsatisfying or unproductive work, dead ends and needless obligation. It could be assortments of worldly things that are cluttering our lives, or maybe He's pruning wrong attitudes like negative thinking, self-hate, jealousy, unforgiveness, regrets, or fear. We don't need any of those foolish interferences which lessen our spiritual fruitfulness.

Don't forget that God is the only One who can do

the pruning successfully—and beneficially. Perhaps you are feeling like you need to quit a job, a relationship with someone, or move out of a certain environment. Before you use your "pruning shears," be sure to submit yourself to God and ask Him to have His way, or you might do great damage to the fruit He has in mind. Sometimes our discomfort in a situation will ultimately produce the fruit of patience or other attributes that will help us to grow in maturity and make our lives better.

We can read in the Old Testament about how the Israelites suffered the consequences of not waiting for the Lord's direction. In one example, they experienced God's anger for not inquiring of Him before proceeding with their own plan.[41]

Since everyone has a limited perspective about what is ahead,[42] nor do we know everything that we will need, it is a wise person who seeks God's counsel before every decision. No matter what that something is, it would be foolish to attempt to make any changes without God's perfect guidance. Incidentally, He is offering it to you right now.

*Call to me and I will answer you. I'll tell you marvelous and wondrous things that you could never figure out on your own (Jeremiah 33:3 MSG).*

Sometimes we see things in others that we think should be pruned. Once again, remember it is not our part to do the clipping. We can be assured that the true Gardner will do the appropriate pruning when the season is right for spiritual health and sanctification.

One dictionary states: "Sanctification is the state of proper functioning."[43] We are sanctified so that we can be used for the purpose God intends—and live accordingly. Pruning is part of the process to help us function properly and make us holy, and it may come when we least expect it. Furthermore, we may not see the cutting as coming from the hand of God. No matter what we think, a mature Christian realizes that God is always working,[44] and remembers that He is working for our good, despite whatever the circumstances may seem to be.

Though it may hurt, the cutting away of the accumulation of fleshly deadness will help us to be free. Neither does dying to oneself feel very good initially, but in the end, the freedom we will experience will be well worth it.

*I consider that our present sufferings are not worth comparing with the glory that will be revealed in us (Romans 8:18 NIV).*

Technically, Jesus Christ has already done all the work to give us deliverance from living in counterproductivity with our baggage. Although I can tell you that the Word teaches us how to get free of all that worthless accumulation, mere instruction isn't enough. It involves making a choice. Until we intentionally *let go* of those constrictive things—leaving them at the Cross—victory is blocked. However, if we sincerely do this by the Grace of God, our Father gently prunes away that which is useless and inhibiting.

*To the Jews who had believed him, Jesus said, "If you hold to my teaching, you are really my disciples. Then you will know the truth, and the truth will set you free" (John 8:31-32 NIV).*

As Jesus spoke of the branches and the pruning, we can see there is a healthy progression of the growth of fruit, the ultimate purpose. John 15:2 shows that when there is fruit, the vinedresser prunes the branch to make it bear more fruit. Then in verse 5, we learn that remaining in Jesus will cause us to bear much fruit. The goal is reached when, according to verse 8, the Father is glorified with *much fruit.*

As "branches," we are expected to produce fruit. It's not an option, and we should know that we will certainly be subject to the Vinedresser's pruning for this to happen. Meanwhile, church attendance and fellowship with our brothers and sisters can encourage us to be productive. It can help keep us in the right mindset regarding this goal so that we do not become discouraged and disheartened. I think the Song of Songs depicts the Lord's gentle voice and tenderness of His love involved in the season of pruning.

*"My beloved responded and said to me, 'Arise, my darling, my beautiful one, And come along. For behold, the winter is past, The rain is over and gone. The flowers have already appeared in the land; The time has arrived for pruning the vines, And the voice of the turtledove has been heard in our land. The fig tree has ripened its figs, And the vines in blossom have given forth their fragrance. Arise, my darling, my beautiful one, And come along!'" (Song of Songs 2:10-13 NASB).*

# CULTIVATING QUESTIONS

## For Chapter 7

1. Who is the Vine and who are the branches?

2. Is there anything worthwhile that we can do if we're not abiding in the Vine? (See John 15:5.)

3. What does Galatians 5:6 indicate that is the only thing that counts?

4. According to Philippians 1:20-21, what did living mean for the apostle Paul?

5. Can you think of something that was once part of your life that has been pruned?

6. Considering your current circumstances, which fruit listed in Galatians 5:22-23 would you especially like to be manifested in your life today?

7. Read Matthew 7:15-20. How can you recognize a Christian?

# Chapter 8

# SEASONS

*To everything there is a season, A time for every purpose under heaven (Ecclesiastes 3:1 NKJV).*

When we look at the word "seasons," we usually think of spring, summer, autumn, and winter, but another way we can think of seasons is as an indefinite period in our lives characterized by a particular feature, such as certain activities, events, or stages. We may experience chapters or phases in our life which are significantly different from what is typical for us.

We've all experienced various seasons, and they may have been pleasant, difficult, gradual or sudden, or they might be described as a fork in the road that sends us in a different direction from the way we were previously going. Perhaps it's a period of learning, new relationships, changes in work or placement, some type of loss, or a time of sickness, to mention a few possibilities. Whatever circumstance, it is God who changes our times and seasons[45], and He does it for His exceptional purposes.

*And we know that all things work together for good to those who love God, to those who are the called according to His purpose (Romans 8:28 NKJV).*

Years ago, there was an unhappy season in my life when I wasn't interested in going to church. I thought there would be too many things I'd have to change, and I wanted to live life doing anything I wanted. I hadn't yet understood God's grace and forgiveness that would truly set me free, and until I changed my mind and chose His better Way, my life was miserable. Perhaps, like me, you can relate to a hard season like that and identify with the following words.

*For day and night your hand was heavy on me; my strength was sapped as in the heat of summer (Psalm 32:4 NIV).*

When, at last, the psalmist David acknowledged his sin and sought the Lord, he was delivered from his wretchedness. I'm happy to tell you that when I finally turned to the Lord for rescue from that futile season of wrong living, I learned that all my sins were forgiven because of the Blood of Jesus.[46] (I think you know by now that I'm quite interested in going to church nowadays.)

The Bible lists many seasons which don't usually pertain to the weather.[47] It is a good idea to consider them:

| a time to be born | a time to die |
|---|---|
| a time to kill | a time to heal |
| a time to tear down | a time to build |
| a time to weep | a time to laugh |
| a time to mourn | a time to dance |
| a time to scatter stones | a time to gather stones |
| a time to plant | a time to uproot |
| a time to embrace | a time to refrain from embracing |

| a time to search | a time to give up |
|---|---|
| a time to keep | a time to throw away |
| a time to tear | a time to mend |
| a time to be silent | a time to speak |
| a time to love | a time to hate |
| a time for war | a time for peace |

There are assorted times in the seasons of everyone's life, and, of course, we find some of them more desirable than others. Though you may have questioned why God allowed certain things to happen, keep trusting Him—even in those dark times that are perceived as hurtful. The Lord wants to use it all to bless you.

*Is it not from the mouth of the Most High that both calamities and good things come? (Lamentations 3:38 NIV).*

Maybe you have gone through a season of calamities. (Other Bible translations use the words *"woe," "hard things"* and *"ill"* instead of the word *"calamities."*) If you haven't experienced these things, I'd be surprised, because sooner or later, everyone goes through them. Of course, calamities don't feel great. Although God does everything for our good, that doesn't mean everything *feels* good. Nevertheless, in due course, God is able to harmonize them together with all His workings for the good of His children.

*Yet God has made everything beautiful for its own time. He has planted eternity in the human heart, but even so, people cannot see the whole scope of God's work from beginning to end (Ecclesiastes 3:11 NLT).*

Even though we don't want to go through a hard season, our view of what is happening is extremely limited. Imagine what would happen to the production of fruit in the world if there was only one season. Farmers know that each season has its value, and without them their crops would be fruitless.

Phrases such as "in the appointed time," "when the set time had fully come," "in the course of time," "proper time," "due time," "time of trouble," "time of prosperity," "until the time," and other wording indicating God's timing, can be found throughout the Bible. His divine timing of seasons cannot, and should not, be ignored.

*Whoever obeys his command will come to no harm, and the wise heart will know the proper time and procedure (Ecclesiastes 8:5 NIV).*

The Israelites repeatedly experienced deliverance from many kinds of difficult circumstances. Unfortunately, they quickly forgot what God had done in the past.[48] If you are in a difficult season, remember to think of the times when He rescued you from past problems and remember His blessings. Ask God to strengthen you and determine to believe that He can surely use the time you are going through for your good.

We may have doubt when our problems seem like they're over our heads, but whenever we think we can take care of things on our own, that's when we'll really find ourselves drowning in impossibilities. We can rejoice that God does the impossible. Meditate on the fact that even the wind and the waves obey Him. He parts the sea, closes the mouths of lions, and brings the dead to life.

*Love never gives up, never loses faith, is always hopeful, and endures through every circumstance (1 Corinthians 13:7 NLT).*

The seasons of our lives will come and go. If you are

in a dark and dreary time of your life, remember that sunshine could be right around the corner. Someday soon, we will be forever rescued from "bad weather." Watch for that day. The climate will certainly change.

*Be on guard! Be alert! You do not know when that time will come (Mark 13:33 NIV).*

Keep watching for that magnificent season. We can prepare ourselves to be ready. Wise King Solomon reminds us in the following verse about that upcoming season with the words with which he reminded himself.

*I said to myself, "In due season God will judge everyone, both good and bad, for all their deeds" (Ecclesiastes 3:17 NLT).*

Meanwhile, before that day of judgment, we have a great promise that God will bless us in every season of our lives as we obey Him. We obey Him by clinging to the Vine, and there is no season where we will be unprotected as we remain in Him.

*How blessed is the man who does not walk in the counsel of the wicked, Nor stand in the path of sinners, Nor sit in the seat of scoffers! But his delight is in the law of the LORD, And in His law he meditates day and night. He will be like a tree firmly planted by streams of water, Which yields its fruit in its season And its leaf does not wither; And in whatever he does, he prospers (Psalm 1:1-3 NASB).*

# CULTIVATING QUESTIONS

## For Chapter 8

1.  Can you identify with a season listed in Ecclesiastes 3:2-8 that you are personally experiencing or have experienced?

2.  Explain why summer, winter, fall or spring best depict the season of life that you are in today.

3.  Read John 15:7-8 and tell what you can do to ensure that your prayers are answered.

4.  Read Philippians 4:4-7. Explain how following these instructions can help you while you're going through a difficult season

5.  According to Nehemiah 8:10, what can give you strength?

6.  According to Genesis 8:22, how can we know that while the earth remains there will continue to be seasons?

7.  What is your most favorite and least favorite weather season? Explain why.

*Chapter 9*

# FRUIT

*But the fruit of the Spirit is love, joy, peace, patience, kindness, goodness, faithfulness, gentleness, self-control; against such things there is no law (Galatians 5:22-23 NASB).*

I've learned that it's helpful for me to take a regular look at the above verse and try to figure out which of the fruit I'm producing—or failing to produce. I keep a list of the fruit of the Spirit in my prayer journal, and when I remember to do it, it's a helpful exercise for me to review the list. Then, I examine myself to see if I have an attitude that particularly needs work. Many times, the Holy Spirit will help me see where I'm especially needy, although, frankly, I don't always like what I'm convicted about. Still, I can then confess my neglect and pray that I will be more fruitful.[49]

None of us see ourselves as clearly as we think we do, but if we humble ourselves and ask the Lord to reveal our shortfalls, He helps us by His reassuring Holy Spirit power. Meanwhile, bearing fruit should always be a high priority for our lives, because it's the Lord's priority for what He wants to see in His children. It's a win-win, as they say, since that's how we can bless God. Plus, the fruit of the Spirit will bring us fulfillment.

I have frequently mentioned our need for abiding in Jesus, and I will continue to emphasize this because of its major importance. Only when we abide in Him will good fruit be produced.

*Live in me. Make your home in me just as I do in you. In the same way that a branch can't bear grapes by itself but only by being joined to the vine, you can't bear fruit unless you are joined with me (John 15:4 MSG).*

I believe we must be joined with other believers in order to get more help in bearing fruit. In my experience, after several weeks of not being able to attend church on Sunday because of pandemic restrictions, I felt a sharp contrast in the difference between tuning in to the worship services at home by myself compared to physical attendance at my church. Metaphorically speaking, if one could feel the moisture of the fruit of the Spirit, I'd say that something juicy happens in the sanctuary that doesn't happen when I sit in front of the computer or tv screen at home. That's because, when Christians gather, the precious fruit of the Spirit is especially manifest.

Not only do I want to have the fruit of the Spirit produced in me, I also enjoy it when it's around me, permeating the air in joint worship. That kind of sharing isn't as available when I'm physically apart from the Body. For various reasons, some people don't have the privilege of leaving their home to attend church services. However, for those who have the choice, it's well worth the effort.

I believe that the ability to produce fruit is transmittable. For instance, do you find it true that when you are around peaceful individuals, you experience more peace? Proverbs 15:12 tells us that peace and gentleness defuse anger. In another Scripture, we learn that the effect of peace is quietness and confidence.[50] Those things are rather valuable in this noisy and often-exasperating world.

What usually happens when you're around loving people who are full of joy and radiant smiles? It's hard to be depressed around people like that. The very sound of heartfelt laughter can bring us a happy feeling. I've noticed that my grandbabies automatically respond with apparent delight to laughter and smiling faces.

In 1 Thessalonians 5:16, the apostle Paul reminds us to continually keep ourselves in joy. That's what Christians are supposed to do, even when we don't especially feel like it—and Paul was a great example.

One day, Paul and Silas were attacked by a crowd of people, stripped, beaten and thrown mercilessly into prison, with their feet placed in painfully uncomfortable stocks. Yet, they began enthusiastically singing and praying, despite their miserable predicament. As it turned out, good things were accomplished through their positive behavior. An earthquake shook the prison to its foundation and the jail doors flew open. (See Acts 16:22-26.)

The fruit of joy, and *all* the fruit of the Spirit, can bring miraculous change to our lives. God is pleased with a good attitude, and He rewards those who are fruitful by abiding in Him. Keep in mind, though, that the best fruit takes time.

Proper ripening on the vine is significant to the taste. Just because the fruit appears ripe, doesn't mean that it is.

Sour grapes aren't appealing. Similarly, insincere people who pretend to have joy or love to influence people, but don't have the power of God, are wasting their time. Bad fruit is like poison to unbelievers—if they have observed phoniness. Sadly, it has caused some to turn away from the Church.

*These are spots in your love feasts, while they feast with you without fear, serving only themselves. They are clouds without water, carried about by the winds; late autumn trees without fruit, twice dead, pulled up by the roots (Jude 1:12 NKJV).*

We have no power without being grounded in Jesus. Have you ever entered a room where you felt something abrasive that you couldn't put your finger on? Have you ever walked into a business or store where you immediately sensed an unwelcoming spirit. Unfortunately, like the fruit of peace, the bad fruit of discord is transmittable, too. The Bible refers to many kinds of bad fruit which come from fleshly living.

*Now the deeds of the flesh are evident, which are: immorality, impurity, sensuality, idolatry, sorcery, enmities, strife, jealousy, outbursts of anger, disputes, dissensions, factions, envying, drunkenness, carousing, and things like these, of which I forewarn you, just as I have forewarned you, that those who practice such things will not inherit the kingdom of God (Galatians 5:19-21 NASB).*

Not only should we consider if there is good fruit in our lives, but we need to be aware of fleshly things, such as bad thoughts, that we may have entertained. These can also affect the spiritual climate of those around us.

*A good tree produces good fruit, and a bad tree produces bad fruit. A good tree can't produce bad fruit, and a bad tree can't produce good fruit. So every tree that does not produce good fruit is chopped down and thrown into the fire. (Matthew 7:17-19 NLT).*

There's a tendency to think that the above verse only refers to the fire of Hell. However, I believe there is a fire of punishment that everyone experiences in this life for the wicked things we think or do without repentance. Sooner or later, everyone reaps what he or she sows.[51] A Christian can expect to be chastised when he or she knowingly continues in disobedience. A father who loves his children will certainly correct them when they display bad behavior.

*For the LORD disciplines those he loves, and he punishes each one he accepts as his child (Hebrews 12:6 NLT).*

We know that the Lord is especially pleased when we show love to each other. We could say that the fruit of love is "the cream of the crop." When Jesus was asked which is the greatest commandment, it was clear that He thought love was the most important thing.[52] One of the ways we demonstrate our love for one another is by being accountable to each other. The church can help us with that area of accountability. Since we are accountable and responsible for each other, it is necessary to have regular meetings. I think that the following admonitions are usually obeyed primarily through the local church.

*Preach the word; be prepared in season and out of season; correct, rebuke and encourage—with great patience and careful instruction (2 Timothy 4:2 NIV).*

The fruit of the Spirit is a marvelous, sharable product found in the Church with which everyone can benefit. All of us should pass it around as much as possible. It's how our Father is glorified.[53] Isn't it amazing that humans, who were made by God, can give glory to Him? It's a remarkable thought that we can give anything to the One who gave us life and breath, the Creator of the universe, the Lord and Ruler of all, but we can bring Him glory right now!

There was something else that Jesus said about fruit which we should think about. He was warning the chief priests and Pharisees about the consequences of those who do not produce fruit.

*Therefore I say to you, the kingdom of God will be taken away from you and given to a people producing the fruit of it (Matthew 21:43 NASB).*

The MSG translation of the same verse says God's kingdom will be handed over *"to a people who will live out a kingdom life."* I appreciate those words, because they appropriate life to those who *live out* a kingdom life. Do you think that kingdom life would include only one or two people, or would it be many citizens who share life under the rule of the king? Whoever heard of an orchard with only a single tree? Surely, kingdom life is shared by many Christians. They will produce much fruit, and in obedience to the King, assemble with their brothers and sisters.

*And let us not neglect our meeting together, as some people do, but encourage one another, especially now that the day of his return is drawing near (Hebrews 10:25 NLT).*

# CULTIVATING QUESTIONS

## For Chapter 9

1. List the fruit of the Spirit.

2. What is the effect of good fruit mentioned in Isaiah 32:17?

3. As seen in John 15:16, what is God's appointment for every Christian?

4. According to Romans 7:4, what does the resurrection of Christ make it possible for us to do?

5. What fruit can calm a quarrel? (See Proverbs 15:18.)

6. Read 1 Peter 3:15–16. What is a fruit that we need when telling others about our hope in Jesus?

7. What fruit covers all wrongs as indicated in Proverbs 10:12?

Chapter 10

# THORNS, THISTLES AND WEEDS

*"The owner's servants came to him and said, 'Sir, didn't you sow good seed in your field? Where then did the weeds come from?' 'An enemy did this,' he replied. The servants asked him, 'Do you want us to go and pull them up?'" 'No,' he answered, 'because while you are pulling the weeds, you may uproot the wheat with them. Let both grow together until the harvest. At that time I will tell the harvesters: First collect the weeds and tie them in bundles to be burned; then gather the wheat and bring it into my barn'" (Matthew 13:27-30 NIV).*

Like many homeowners, I've fought the battle against crab grass, dandelions, brown grass and the like since my first involvement in keeping a yard. Even as a child, I remember the chore of digging up and plucking out the weeds that could choke the desirable plants.

Anyone who has had any experience gardening knows about those ugly intruders that grow so easily between the vegetable plants and between the cherished flowers. They make a garden look unkempt and messy, and they can also spoil the appearance of a lawn, growing disturbingly fast where you don't want them.

In the above parable, Jesus used the image of weeds to illustrate worldliness and sin. While we live in the world, we will find these things will show up where we don't want them.

*This is what the LORD says to the people of Judah and Jerusalem: "Plow up the hard ground of your hearts! Do not waste your good seed among thorns" (Jeremiah 4:3 NLT).*

The NKJV translates that verse as, *"Break up your fallow ground."* Fallow ground is soil that has been uncultivated for a long time and has likely been abandoned to weeds. We need to look at those fallow areas in our lives that we have ignored. If we let things go too long without plowing, the task will become more difficult to eliminate the undesired growth.

Sometimes a weed can appear to be a flower, or even something edible, but when examined closely we find it may badly affect the growth of other plants, be harmful to eat, or even touch. Jesus warned us about disguises in people and the need for discernment, so we won't be hurt.

*Beware of the false prophets, who come to you in sheep's clothing, but inwardly are ravenous wolves (Matthew 7:15 NASB).*

God gives us discernment through His Holy Spirit. As we renew our minds and receive the Word of God, we will grow in knowledge and understanding so that we will be able to distinguish good and evil by testing the spirits.[54]

One street in the city where I live has an uncommon number of churches within a couple of blocks. However, just because they look like churches on the outside, doesn't mean that they are teaching the truth.

The Bible tells us about the wicked King Ahaz who religiously made altars in every corner of Jerusalem.[55] Yet, he was not led by the Lord, and it made God very angry. Although there may be plentiful church buildings on every corner in our towns, religions without Jesus are like tares the devil sows.

There are many kinds of harmful plants that grow throughout the world. One common example is poison ivy. It doesn't look that threatening, but you better not touch it. The enemy sows misery in many forms. For instance, the presence of weeds usually indicates neglect in one form or another.

*I went by the field of the lazy man, And by the vineyard of the man devoid of understanding; And there it was, all overgrown with thorns; Its surface was covered with nettles; Its stone wall was broken down. When I saw it, I considered it well; I looked on it and received instruction: A little sleep, a little slumber, A little folding of the hands to rest; So shall your poverty come like a prowler, And your need like an armed man (Proverbs 24:30-34).*

Those who carelessly forsake the Lord can be compared to a dried-up garden.[56] Unlike the field of the lazy man described in the above verse, our lives will not be overgrown with poverty and despair if we maintain the garden of our hearts.

*This is what the LORD says: "Maintain justice and do what is right, for my salvation is close at hand and my righteousness will soon be revealed (Isaiah 56:1 NIV).*

Weeds are a serious concern for the farmer, and the Vinedresser has given us a part in maintenance. Upkeep isn't a one-time thing—like being born again—it must be a regular endeavor.

Once we are spiritually reborn, this doesn't have to be done repeatedly, because this is done when Jesus becomes our Savior. Nevertheless, we do need to continually work at keeping our lives clean. There is labor involved, as the apostle Paul indicated.

*Therefore, my dear friends, as you have always obeyed not only in my presence, but now much more in my absence, continue to work out your salvation with fear and trembling (Philippians 2:12 NIV).*

One of many examples suggesting the need for maintenance was when God told the Israelites to *consecrate* themselves. (See Leviticus 20:7–8.) In the dictionary, the word consecrate is defined as "To set apart as holy."[57] That command has never changed. Biblical writers reiterated that need for us using many words, such as the reminder in the following verse.

*Therefore, having these promises, beloved, let us cleanse ourselves from all defilement of flesh and spirit, perfecting holiness in the fear of God (2 Corinthians 7:1 NASB).*

We are being made holy,[58] and keeping ourselves pure from the infiltration of sin is a basic principle of Christianity. Some individuals are apparently passively waiting for Heaven, and they are not conscientiously exterminating the weeds or keeping brambles from taking over. Perhaps they don't remember that *now* is the day of salvation.[59] That's every day as we look forward to our ultimate rescue in the future.

*Each tree is recognized by its own fruit. People do not pick figs from thornbushes, or grapes from briers (Luke 6:44 NIV).*

Horticulturists tell us how to identify weeds, and they categorize them as perennials, annuals, or biennials. Perennial weeds are probably the hardest to remove, because they have long taproots. Annual weeds are frustrating because they grow every year in different places, and biennials produce flowers in the first year and seeds in their second year. Perhaps you will see some similarities regarding the nature of these weeds in the spiritual sense to which I have been referring. In the parable of the tares, Jesus spoke about how weeds can dreadfully strangle a plant.

*And the seed that fell in the weeds—well, these are the ones who hear, but then the seed is crowded out and nothing comes of it as they go about their lives worrying about tomorrow, making money, and having fun. (Luke 8:14 MSG).*

Negative words and thoughts can be compared to weeds. If allowed to grow, they will wreck the possibility of a fruitful harvest. In Hosea 10:4, the prophet warned against empty words that spring up like poisonous weeds in a farmer's field.

Motivational speaker and writer, Jim Rohn, wrote, "You cannot take the mild approach to the weeds in your mental garden. You have got to hate weeds enough to kill them. Weeds are not something you handle; weeds are something you devastate."[60]

Through my personal gardening experience, I've learned that careless weeding doesn't take care of the problem. Weeds must be eradicated—not just a mere topical raking that removes only the displeasing, visible weed heads, but rather a deep digging to remove the roots—or the weeds will surely sprout again.

There are many tasks that must be performed to do the job right. For instance, I can sweep the dust and dirt under the furniture, but that won't make the house clean, and I better not have any decadent desserts in the refrigerator or the pantry if I'm trying to lose weight. A recovering alcoholic knows better than to keep any liquor in the house.

Those are only a few comparisons, and you can probably think of more, but like weeds, those kinds of things must be eliminated for success in our pursuits, and if they aren't removed, it will be easier for the enemy of our souls to overrun and invade us.

*Don't let down your guard lest even now, today, someone—man or woman, clan or tribe—gets sidetracked from GOD, our God, and gets involved with the no-gods of the nations; lest some poisonous weed sprout and spread among you (Deuteronomy 29:18 MSG).*

Throughout the Bible, we see repeated warnings about the great danger of allowing impurities, like weeds, to infest our lives. Even the smallest root of sin can inhibit our effectiveness and spiritual beauty.

Back when the world was in its earliest stages, God warned Cain about the poisonous weed of sin and the need to rule over it before it cropped up.

*If you do what is right, will you not be accepted? But if you do not do what is right, sin is crouching at your door; it desires to have you, but you must rule over it (Genesis 4:7 NIV).*

Unfortunately, Cain didn't rule over a bitter root of envy. Instead of guarding his heart, he lost control, and he murdered Abel, his brother. Cain's lack of self-control is an example for us, showing that we must rule over the weeds of sin so that they don't overtake us. As we join with others in church fellowship who are also fighting for weed control, we can all have more protection from invasion through our joint efforts.

*Sow righteousness for yourselves, reap the fruit of unfailing love, and break up your **unplowed ground;** for it is time to seek the L*ORD*, until he comes and showers his righteousness on you (Hosea 10:12 NIV; emphasis added).*

# CULTIVATING QUESTIONS

## For Chapter 10

1.  Why is discernment so important to your growth and life? (See Philippians 1: 9-10.)

2.  According to Hebrews 12:15, what does a root of bitterness do to a person?

3.  Read Psalm 92:12-13. Where should the righteous be planted so that they may flourish?

4.  Norman Vincent Peale said, "Dwelling on negative thoughts is like fertilizing weeds."[61] What do you think he meant?

5.  Give an example of something that needs to be eradicated from your life in order to have victory.

6.  What kind of people should those who pursue righteousness try to be around? (See 2 Timothy 2:22.)

7.  What is the only way anyone can be purified from sin? (See 1 John 1:7.)

*Chapter 11*

# FIRE

*The Son of Man will send out his angels, and they will weed out of his kingdom everything that causes sin and all who do evil. They will throw them into the blazing furnace, where there will be weeping and gnashing of teeth. Then the righteous will shine like the sun in the kingdom of their Father. Whoever has ears, let them hear (Matthew 13:41-43 NIV).*

I debated with myself about using this subject as a chapter for this book. Like others who share the Gospel, I want to encourage people rather than bring doom and dismay. So, there's a tendency to avoid the dreadful subject of the fire of Hell. Nevertheless, the Bible tells us in no uncertain terms that it is the ultimate destination of those who refuse to repent and continue to do evil. We must not ignore the many warnings—and people must be told.

The "hellfire and brimstone" preachers of the past might be appalled at our hesitation to speak of Hell. Some of us remember how they shouted warning without mincing words, emphasizing the terrible danger of judgment and eternal punishment. However shocking,

I believe that in those days of their fervent evangelism, some people were converted by fear.

*Knowing, therefore, the terror of the Lord, we persuade men; but we are well known to God, and I also trust are well known in your consciences (2 Corinthians 5:11 NKJV).*

Surely, those earlier preachers would be dismayed to see how the evil in the world has progressed. The apostle Paul wrote to Timothy about how the behavior of people would be in the end times, and his words depict the attitudes of what is going on in our world today.

*But realize this, that in the last days difficult times will come. For men will be lovers of self, lovers of money, boastful, arrogant, revilers, disobedient to parents, ungrateful, unholy, unloving, irreconcilable, malicious gossips, without self-control, brutal, haters of good, treacherous, reckless, conceited, lovers of pleasure rather than lovers of God (2 Timothy 3:1-4 NASB).*

Most people, and apparently many Christians, have become desensitized to evil. Could one reason be that words of caution have been unspoken or diluted? If nobody wants to speak of an eternal penalty, and sin is tolerated and ignored without mentioning punishment, it's not surprising that wickedness would multiply. In 2 Timothy 4:1-2, we are given the charge to proclaim the Word. Surely, that doesn't mean that we should pick and choose only what's comfortable to share—or hear.

Sometimes, we Christians treat those who are living in obvious sin as if they are too fragile to hear the truth, but it might be *we* who are too fragile. We don't want to hear people tell us we are judgmental or self-righteous when we address the wrongs that the Bible tells us are unacceptable. Are we caring more about what people think than what God wants? I fear that we Christians have permitted too much without voicing the truth.

To mention only a few examples, deplorable participation in things forbidden by God, such as homosexuality, sexually promiscuous relationships (both homosexual and heterosexual), and abortion are commonplace in the world today. If anyone dares to state that someone is choosing the road to perdition, they can usually expect to be ruthlessly criticized. Believers who refuse to compromise the truth will suffer the contempt of the enemies of God.

Perhaps that growing monster—political correctness— that so many bow to or shrink back from, has inhibited our voice. Nevertheless, the Word of God should be upheld even when it is contradicted by the loud, demonic voices of those contradicting it.

*And you, son of man, neither fear them nor fear their words, though thistles and thorns are with you and you sit on scorpions; neither fear their words nor be dismayed at their presence, for they are a rebellious house. But you shall speak My words to them whether they listen or not, for they are rebellious (Ezekiel 2:6-7 NASB).*

Michael L. White wrote the following words in his outstanding book, *The Salvation of the Lord:* "It is intriguing to me that so many of those who classify themselves as atheists or agnostics (and a shocking number of professing Christians, too) like to scorn the Biblical teaching and preaching about Hell and divine judgment. They point out how unjust or unloving they think it would be for God to create such a place as Hell, let alone to condemn anyone to spend eternity there. In response to their misunderstanding, let me clarify that, although God did indeed create a place of punishment called Hell, He doesn't condemn or send *any human being* there without first offering them the opportunity to escape it—*multiple times*. Therefore, by providing a means of escape from Hell and offering it to every person who ever lives, it is each individual's own choice to go to Hell when he or she rejects God's Plan of Salvation."[62]

I think that people who reject God's Plan of Salvation are usually also the ones who detest the Church and organized religion, but why in the world do they think that organized religion is so terrible? I think they want their homes, their possessions, their finances, the government and our defense organized, don't they? Obviously, the devil doesn't want our religion to be organized.

Furthermore, I believe the number one reason that those same people do not like church is because the conviction of the Holy Spirit is much too uncomfortable and hard to ignore.

*And when He has come, He will convict the world of sin, and of righteousness, and of judgment: of sin, because they do not believe in Me (John 16:8-9 NKJV).*

The Church is full of the glorious Light of the Holy Spirit. Light exposes darkness, and the glare of the truth can indeed be painful to sinners. In fact, every born-again Christian has truly experienced that excruciating pain of recognizing the blackness of one's own heart. It brought us to repentance and acknowledgement of our great need for the Savior, Jesus Christ.

*Then you will remember your evil ways and your deeds that were not good; and you will loathe yourselves in your own sight, for your iniquities and your abominations (Ezekiel 36:31 NKJV).*

I believe there are a lot more people who believe in God than there are atheists. However, it's not enough to know the truth. James 2:19 indicates that even the demons believe, but demons are prideful, not humble. Jesus said only a few people find the narrow road that leads to life[63]—and pride is a major obstacle. Determining to humble ourselves and admit our need for forgiveness is essential to finding that blessed, narrow road to life, but the cost of humility is too high for some.

*Therefore, as the fire devours the stubble, And the flame consumes the chaff, So their root will be as rottenness, And their blossom will ascend like dust; Because they have rejected the law of the LORD of hosts, And despised the word of the Holy One of Israel (Isaiah 5:24 NKJV).*

The Bible tells us that truth is clearly seen and that people are without excuse for disbelieving God.[64] In the modern world of technology, information on any subject is available, including the Word of God, and it is offered through books, television and the internet, among other sources, Yet, people usually choose the subject matter that appeals to the flesh.

*And what do you benefit if you gain the whole world but lose your own soul? Is anything worth more than your soul? (Matthew 16:26 NLT).*

Jesus Christ was born to save our souls and has given everyone the opportunity to trade their *heart of stone* for His *heart of flesh* to be born within them. (See Ezekiel 36:26.) If you have not been born again and received the life of Jesus within you, don't wait a minute longer. Repent of your sin and ask God to save you.

*Whoever has the Son **has life;** whoever does not have God's Son does not have life (1 John 5:12 NLT; emphasis added).*

The lake of fire, noted in Revelation 20:15, is the eternal destination of those who have not received Him. Along with Old Testament prophets and other godly men, the apostle Paul wrote many warnings. Consider the following warning from him.

*Dear friends, if we deliberately continue sinning after we have received knowledge of the truth, there is no longer any sacrifice that will cover these sins. There is only the terrible expectation of God's judgment and the raging fire that will consume his enemies (Hebrews 10:26-27 NLT).*

# CULTIVATING QUESTIONS

## For Chapter 11

1.  Read Matthew 10:28 and tell what people should fear.

2.  Who is it that the apostle Paul warns us not to refuse in Hebrews 12:25-28?

3.  For how long are those who hate the Lord to be punished? (See Psalm 81:15.)

4.  What is an attitude towards a brother or sister that could mean the fire of Hell if not corrected? (See Matthew 5:22.)

5.  What do you think the light has to do with Christian fellowship according to 1 John 1:7?

6.  To whom is the message in 2 Chronicles 7:14 specifically given?

7.  Read Isaiah 53:5-6. What keeps Christians free from the punishment of Hell?

*Chapter 12*

# HARVEST

*And another angel came out from the altar, who had power over fire, and he cried with a loud cry to him who had the sharp sickle, saying, "Thrust in your sharp sickle and gather the clusters of the vine of the earth, for her grapes are fully ripe" (Revelation 14:18 NKJV).*

The book of Revelation has a lot to say about the end time, and particularly about the time of harvest. The fruit that is produced and is finally *"ripe"* is what that's all about. As we wait for that inevitable day, we can get ready for it by being fruitful in our thoughts, words and actions.

Jesus often spoke about the harvest. He referred to the harvest as being the end of the world and referred to the harvest of souls.[65] The harvest was a particularly important time for the Hebrew people, because it was a season in which they received their food supply. Nowadays, unless someone is directly involved in agricultural work, we are far removed from the actual harvesting, and we don't pay much attention to it. Instead, we depend on what's available at the grocery store.

The harvest of our spiritual fruit is another matter.

The Church is where the good fruit will be found at harvest time. To ensure that we are not separated from the Body of Christ, we need to be rooted and grounded *with all the saints,*[66] because separation from the saints (i.e., the Church) also means separation from the Vine.

*"I am the Vine, you are the branches. When you're joined with me and I with you, the relation intimate and organic, the harvest is sure to be abundant. Separated, you can't produce a thing (John 15:5 MSG).*

Abiding in Jesus is where we need to be, all the time, but maybe you're like me. Sometimes, on Sunday mornings, you feel like rolling over and going back to sleep when the alarm clock rings, reminding you to get ready for church. Yet, I know when I discipline myself to be in the house of God each week, I am happier, and I am strengthened to face the coming days.

*Splendor and majesty are before Him, Strength and joy are in His place (1 Chronicles 16:27 NASB).*

I'm grateful that church attendance is a discipline that I was taught when I was a child. My dad and mom made up their minds that our family would go to church each week without question. We didn't have to decide if we were going to get ready for church on Sunday. Thanks to Godly parents, it was rooted in our lifestyle to help us to live fruitfully, even though during my younger years I wasn't so very happy about it.

*No discipline seems pleasant at the time, but painful. Later on, however, it produces a harvest of righteousness and peace for those who have been trained by it (Hebrews 12:11 NIV).*

Even if you don't feel especially enthusiastic about getting up and going to church, remember that your diligence in church attendance can help you develop eternal values and prepare you for that end harvest. Biblical preaching and teaching increase one's power to live and produce fruit. Plus, our faith is built from hearing the Word of God. [67]

We are blessed with having the freedom of religion in America. Christian churches are not so available in some countries. I believe that perseverance in attendance and wholehearted dedication to the local church is compulsory for us because of this blessing.[68] Furthermore, perhaps nothing is quite as fatal to the freedom of Christianity as indifference about attending church.

Keep in mind that there are two harvests which are described in the Bible, and we all need to prioritize getting ready for that unavoidable time. In Chapter 11 of this book, I described the end harvest for those who have rejected Christ, but those who have received Jesus as Savior and Lord will be saved from hell and rewarded for their faithfulness.

*Remember that the Lord will give you an inheritance as your reward, and that the Master you are serving is Christ. But if you do what is wrong, you will be paid back for the wrong you have done. For God has no favorites (Colossians 3:24-25 NLT).*

God has offered the same gift of life to everyone,[69] and every person must choose whether to take it. What decision have you made? Those who haven't received life have already chosen the consequences of the bad harvest, but those who have chosen to receive the greatest gift[70] that has ever been given are rescued.

*And the testimony is this, that God has given us eternal life, and this life is in His Son (1 John 5:11 NASB).*

God has a plan to keep us flourishing and ready for that harvest day, and having our placement in a church home is part of His plan for every believer. Rick Warren wrote, "You must be connected to a church fellowship to survive spiritually."[71] Christians have great need of each other for proper functioning and for survival.

*But our bodies have many parts, and God has put each part just where he wants it. How strange a body would be if it had only one part! Yes, there are many parts, but only one body. The eye can never say to the hand, "I don't need you." The head can't say to the feet, "I don't need you" (1 Corinthians 12:18-21 NLT).*

Corporate worship brings us together so we may have a healthy Body, and we assemble in obedience to God. Although there may be times where we can't meet for one reason or another (such as health considerations, bad weather or other reasons), we should try not to miss opportunities to be with fellow believers.

Again, there will surely be a reward for those people who have been faithful to the Body of Christ. The apostle Paul wrote about how we build on this foundation of the household of God. (See Ephesians 2:19-21). True builders will determine to work together and build, and they will be paid accordingly.[72]

There is a lovely video I've watched on television in December, around Christmas time, that continually shows a holiday scene with a beautiful fireplace burning. I can imagine that I'm feeling the heat of the flames and smelling the smoky scent of the glowing logs. Of course, it's not like really being in a cozy room with a fireplace. I heard someone say that "Online church is like watching that video of a fireplace burning." You see it, but you don't get warm. Similarly, believers require the warmth of Christian fellowship just as fruit requires the heat of the sun to develop properly for harvest. However, the benefits are lost without the source requirement.

In conclusion, I pray that you will be inspired by the words in this book, and that you, dear brothers and sisters, will be well warmed in the church of God's choice for you. If you don't presently have a local church you call "home," pray for God to lead you to one. That is a prayer He is certain to grant.

*Let the peace of Christ keep you in tune with each other, in step with each other. None of this going off and doing your own thing. And cultivate thankfulness (Colossians 3:15 MSG).*

# CULTIVATING QUESTIONS

### For Chapter 12

1. How can you increase your faith? (See Romans 10:17)

2. How is Matthew 18:19-20 especially significant to Christians when meeting together?

3. What does Romans 2:7 say that we need to persist in doing, and why is perseverance so important?

4. What problem do we all have in common with every person on earth? (See Romans 3:23.)

5. Read 1 Thessalonians 4:16-18. What is the comfort in these words for you?

6. Read Luke 12:38-40 and list at least one thing you would do to prepare if you knew Jesus was coming next month.

7. Explain in your own words how anyone can escape God's punishment for sin. (See Ephesians 2:8 and John 3:16.)

# Endnotes

1  http://srv1.worldometers.info/coronavirus/coronavirus-cases
2  https://statista.com/chart/3534/americans-are-tired-most-of-the-week/
3  https://pubmed.ncbi.nlm.nih.gov/21843744
4  https://coffeenatics.com/expert-tips/coffee-consumption-in-the-us
5  See 1 Corinthians 11:18, 11:20, 11:34 and 14:26.
6  Catherine Marshall, *The Helper, p. 164. Part 6,* "Has My Church the Spirit?" (Avon Books, 1978)
7  A message given by Rev. Tim Curtis, used by his permission.
8  A radiant face: Exodus 34:30
9  Jonathan Leeman, *Rediscover Church,* p. 48. "Do We Really Need To Gather?" (Crossway, 2021)
10  Why God must be the builder: Psalm 127:1
11  You are God's building: 1 Corinthians 3:9
12  Prayer to know God: Ephesians 1:17
13  For joy: John 15:9-12
14  Blessed through Abraham: Genesis 18:18
15  No partiality with God: Romans 2:11
16  What's important: Galatians 5:6
17  God's thoughts and ways are far greater: Isaiah 55:8-9
18  The date isn't given: Acts 1:7
19  No one knows when: Matthew 24:36
20  Who is the Vinedresser: John 15:1
21  He wants no one to perish: Matthew 18:14 and 2 Peter 3:9

22  Webster's New College Dictionary, p. 1210, Wiley Publishing Inc., 2005

23  Those that deceive: Mark 13:22-23

24  We can't comprehend everything: Ecclesiastes 8:17

25  Why unity: John 17:23

26  Tony Evans, *Winning Your Spiritual Battles,* p. 31, chapter 2, (Harvest House Publishers, 2019)

27  Best commandment: Mark 12:28-31

28  Those who don't wither: Psalm 1:2-3

29  Our enemies: Ephesians 6:12

30  Loneliness described: Psalm 102:7 (NLT)

31  Godliness is more profitable: 1 Timothy 4:8

32  The fruit of the Spirit listed in Galatians 5:22-23

33  Dr. Phil McGraw wrote in the foreword of the book, "Reposition Yourself," by T.D. Jakes, (Atria Books, 2007)

34  We can do nothing without Jesus: John 15:5

35  The devil knows scripture: Matthew 4:6

36  Elizabeth Elliot, *Through Gates of Splendor,* p.20, chapter 1, (Harper & Brothers, 1957)

37  How we are enabled to live: 1 John 4:9

38  Living in love: 1 John 4:16

39  Those who really love the Father: 1 John 5:1

40  Destination of hypocrites: Matthew 24:51

41  When not consulting the Lord: 1 Chronicles 15:13

42  You don't know what will happen tomorrow: Proverbs 27:1

43  https://www.biblestudytools.com/dictionary/sanctification

44  Who never stops working: John 5:17

45  God changes times and seasons: Daniel 2:21

46  What is needed for forgiveness: Hebrews 9:22

47  What times we can expect: Ecclesiastes 3:2-8

48  They forgot what God had done: Psalm 106: 13-15

49  How to get rid of our bad fruit: 1 John 1:9

50  Fruit for quiet confidence: Isaiah 32:17

51  You will get back what you give: Galatians 6:7

52  The most important thing: Matthew 22:37-40

53  How God is glorified: John 15:8

54  Don't believe everything you hear: 1 John 4:1

55  Altars on every corner: 2 Chronicles 28:24

56  What those who forsake God are like: Isaiah 1:30

57  Webster's New College Dictionary, p. 310, Wiley Publishing Inc., 2005

58  How you are made holy: Hebrews 10:14

59  When is Salvation: 2 Corinthians 6:1-2

60  https://www.azquotes.com/quote/823237

61  https://minimalistquotes.com/norman-vincent-peale-quote-147249

62  Michael L. White, *The Salvation of the Lord,* p. 171 (Parson Place Press, 2023).

63  Gateway to life: Matthew 7:14

64  No excuse: Romans 1:20-21

65  Jesus referred to the harvest in Matthew 9:37, Mark 4:29 and John 4:35.

66  Rooted in love: Ephesians 3:17-19

67  Where to get faith: Romans 10:17

68  More is required by those who are given much: Luke 12:48

69  Wages vs. gift: Romans 6:23

70  Forgiveness: Acts 10:43

71  Rick Warren, *Better Together,* Day 15, p. 69 (Purpose Driven Publishing,2007).

72  Results of the builder's work: 1 Corinthians 3:12-15

Printed in the United States
by Baker & Taylor Publisher Services